Discover the Trees

By **Jerry Cowle**
illustrations by **Mike Anderson**

 STERLING PUBLISHING CO., INC. NEW YORK

Contents

Copyright © 1977 by Sterling Publishing Co., Inc.
419 Park Avenue South, New York, N.Y. 10016
Manufactured in the United States of America
Library of Congress Catalog Card No.: 76-51174
Sterling ISBN 0-8069-3734-3 Trade
3735-1 Library

327427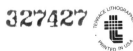

This book is dedicated with love
to
Betty, Ed, Jay, Sally, Suzi, Jennie, and Robbie

Meet the Trees

This is a book of fun. In it, you'll learn many different things about the trees around us. Your friends and even your parents may not know some of them.

If you have trouble finding or identifying a certain tree, it may be because it doesn't grow in your part of the world. Or perhaps you don't recognize it when you see it. You can always ask a park ranger, forest ranger, or county farm agent about trees. They will be happy to answer your questions.

A good part of the fun will be when you discover a new tree. First identify all the trees in your neighborhood. Then look for more trees in other parts of the city or town where you live. When your family takes trips—near or far—bring along this book to help you recognize new trees not in your neighborhood. There are trees wherever you go — over a thousand different species in the United States alone!

Trees are the largest plants in the world. They never stop growing as long as they live. All your life, you'll be living with trees. America's history is interwoven with incidents relating to trees. Our water supply, our food, shelter and clothing are largely dependent on trees or the lack of trees. Try to imagine a world without trees. Can you?

Trees are to enjoy. And now is a fine time to get started. Read on, and have fun!

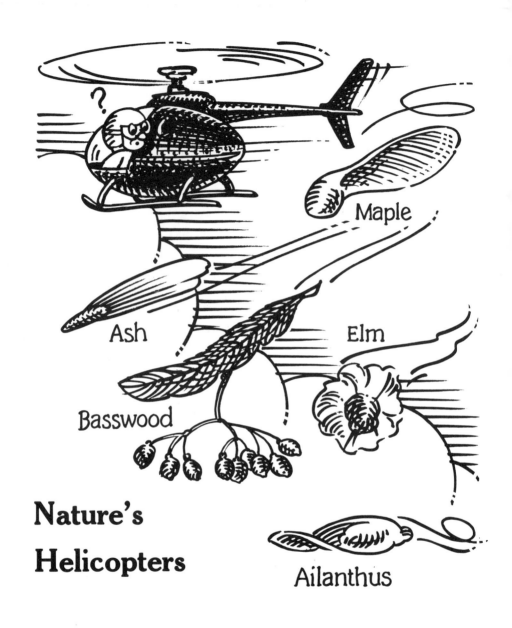

Maple

Ash

Elm

Basswood

Nature's
Helicopters

Ailanthus

Look for the winged seeds of Maple. These are also called winged fruits or samaras. They come in pairs, each with its own wing. Together they look

MOTHER NATURE'S BAG OF TRICKS

like a bird in flight, or a modern jet liner. When they split, they twirl to the ground, looking like a helicopter landing. Try it yourself.

Ash seeds twirl too, but faster. Because they are shaped like canoe paddles.

Look for Elm winged seeds. They look like the kind of pill your doctor gives you that is surrounded by a circle of cellophane. Others think they look like the waterwings that some children learn to swim with.

Look for Basswood. It has a sail leaf with its fruit hanging below. It looks like a giant flying machine that might have been designed by a mad scientist.

Look for Willow seeds, with their fluff on each seed. They're carried by the wind, like toy balloons!

Look for Tree of Heaven seeds *(Ailanthus)*. They look like two-bladed airplane propellers, and they spin through the air when they drop to the ground. (Tree of Heaven is the one that grows even in the deepest parts of the city, where you'd think nothing would grow. It has big leaves, lush and green. But don't crush them, as they don't smell very nice!)

Nature's Popgun

If you live in the eastern half of the United States, look for the Witch Hazel tree, sometimes called Snapping Hazelnut. The cold of late Autumn dries out its tough, powerful nuts. When they're good and ripe and dry, they explode, shooting out two shiny black seeds that are shaped like tiny footballs. These seeds have been known to fly through the air as far as 30 feet, and always at least 10 feet!

Sometimes you can make them explode by touching them. If you take the nuts home and keep them in your room, you'll get a real surprise when they open! The open nut husks look like the hungry mouths of baby robins!

Ask your dad if he has ever used Witch Hazel lotion after shaving. He'll probably say yes. If he has some, smell it. But don't get *too* close. It's good, but strong!

Nature's Picket Fence

Nature gives a tree what it needs for protection. In the case of the Shagbark Hickory, whose nuts are thin-shelled and delicious, Nature had to keep the squirrels from eating every last nut. Otherwise, this wonderful tree might have become extinct.

That's why Shagbark Hickory has shaggy bark. In a way, the bark strips look like those flat, curled leaves that stick out of a fresh pineapple, only upside down. These long gray strips help to keep the hungry squirrels from climbing the tree. And this is even more amazing—the Shagbark Hickory doesn't need this protection until nuts start growing. So, when the tree is young, the bark is smooth. But when the tree gets old enough to grow nuts, then the bark forms the picket fence that tells the squirrels, "KEEP OUT!"

Nature's Medicine Chest

You can find a lot of things to make you feel better when you're in the woods, with no drugstore on the corner. The sticky goo you get when you break the bark blisters of Balsam Fir is a good salve for cuts. (Break a blister on your Balsam Christmas Tree and see!)

Slippery Elm inner bark, when boiled down in water, makes a good cough medicine. The leftover pulp is good to put on sores. For a sore throat, just chew Slippery Elm buds and twigs.

Sassafras root tea is good for a stomach-ache. If you need a laxative, try Black Cherry twig tea. A tea made from Alder leaves is a fine skin wash for pimples.

Chewing on the bark of the Toothache Tree, otherwise called Pepperwood, relieves a toothache. (It only grows in swamps in the South.)

If some of these sound funny, don't laugh. Ask your druggist, and you'll be surprised how many of these old-time woods remedies are actually used in our modern medicines.

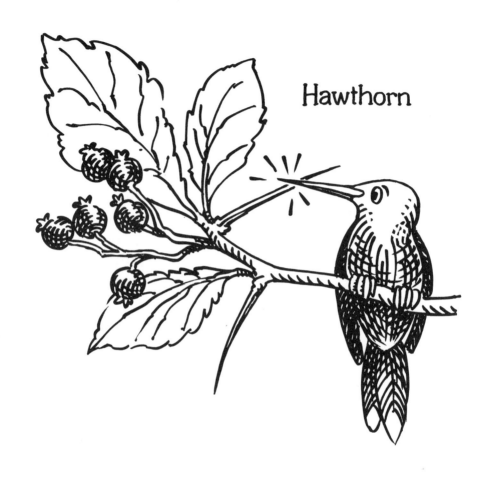

Hawthorn

Nature's Daggers

Here are three trees you wouldn't want to stumble into on a dark night! Their thorns are from 1 to 8 inches in length.

The Hawthorn, sometimes known as Thorn Apple, denotes a number of species that grow in fields all over the United States except in the desert. They have long, sharp thorns, some of which grow as long as 8 inches. No wonder birds feel safe in building their nests in Hawthorn trees. What cat or boy or even hawk would dare to come after them there?

Honey Locust, mostly an eastern and Mississippi Valley tree, has 4-inch needles. Some of them are in the form of three-pronged daggers. It's no fun climbing this one either!

Osage Orange, a southern tree, was transplanted up north by cattlemen in the days before the invention of barbed wire fencing! Planted close together, these trees kept cattle in or out, as the case might be.

If you're ever stuck in the woods with thread, but no needle, you could use one of Nature's daggers if necessary. It might be easier, though, to save the rip for Mother's sewing machine!

Nature's Paint Box

Trees are always beautiful, even in the Winter without their leaves. But in glorious Autumn, between Columbus Day and Halloween, Mother Nature gets out her paints, and the forests burst out in a riot of color.

Wherever you live in America the Beautiful, you'll find at least some of these trees with their coats of color. So take a walk along the street, in the park, or in the woods, and enjoy yourself! Here's what to look for:

FLAME RED, ORANGE...
Sugar Maple, Sumac

WINE RED...
Sweet Gum

PURPLE RED...
Sassafras, Red Maple, Dogwood, Scarlet Oak

GOLDEN YELLOW...
Tulip Tree, Poplar, Birch, Willow, Sassafras

PURPLE...
White Ash, Black Ash

TAN and BROWN...
Oak, Beech, Elm, Hickory, Sycamore

And don't forget the Greens, Blue-Greens, and Yellow-Greens of the Pines, Spruces, Firs, Hemlocks, Cedars, and Yews!

Sweet Gum

Dogwood

Sycamore

Birch

Sugar Maple

Black Ash

A

B

Nature's Costume-Changer

The famous American Sycamore or Button Ball Tree sheds its outer bark every year, just as a snake sheds its skin, then puts on a new costume. Sunlight works on the bark chemicals, making all sorts of interesting patchwork designs in white, purple, gray, green, gold, and brown. The reason this happens is that the outer bark doesn't keep growing. Thus the tree outgrows its clothing, just as you grow out of yours.

Sycamore grows all through the East and Midwest, and is wonderful for grimy cities, because it has an annual cleaning of its "skin"!

It is one of the easiest trees to identify in the Wintertime, because its fruit is 1 inch in diameter, and looks like a ball dangling on a string. Between these button balls and the patchwork-quilt bark, you should find it very easy to recognize Nature's Costume-Changer.

There are also California and Arizona Sycamores which resemble the American Sycamore, except that they have a string of three or more button balls in a group, instead of single ones.

Mr. Knobcone

Nature's Thermostat

Lodgepole Pine, which grows in our Pacific Northwest states, has tightly closed cones that hang for years without opening. Then, when a fire comes through and kills this thin-barked pine, Nature steps in. The fire causes the cones to open, scattering seeds to reforest the burned area. And that's how Lodgepole Pine lives on and on, despite fires.

18

Knobcone Pine is even tougher. Its rock-hard cones can hold seeds for up to *fifty* years, until a fire opens them.

Doesn't it remind you of Sleeping Beauty, who couldn't wake up until the Handsome Prince kissed her?

In the Midwest, Jack Pine has the same type of cones.

Someday, if you can, bring home a Lodgepole Pine or a Jack Pine cone. Then, when you have a fire in the fireplace, try out Nature's Thermostat.

Before Fire—
Closed

After Fire—
Open

Nature's Water Detective

The same Witch Hazel that is Nature's Popgun is also her Water Detective. In the days of the pioneers, people cut a forked Witch Hazel stick from a tree. The person who was looking for water would hold onto both ends of the fork with his hands, and walk along with the stem of the branch pointing straight ahead. If something pulled the end of the branch down, that was where the water was! They'd stop and mark the spot, and dig their well right there. Amazingly enough, there usually *was* water there.

This was called the art of Dowsing. There are still people around, especially in the New England states, who learned the art from their fathers and grandfathers. They insist it really works. Other people scoff at it, and claim that you might find water wherever you dug, if you'd only dig deep enough. What do you think?

20

22

Nature's Fireproof Trees

That's right. Don't worry about the Redwoods and the Big Trees, those huge Sequoia twins of the West Coast, burning down!

The Redwood has bark a full foot thick, and Big Tree's bark grows up to 2 feet thick. What's more, there's no resin inside it to burn like in other trees. And that means fire never even gets a chance to start. They're practically fireproof. Also, the bark is so loaded with tannin that they're practically immune to insect damage. (Tannin is used to make inks and medicines, so you can imagine why insects don't go near it.) No wonder these giant trees live so long!

Nobody cuts down Big Trees anymore, as the Federal Government protects them. But California Coast Redwood is cut for lumber in certain areas. And its fireproof bark is shredded and used to insulate the walls of houses.

Sing-Along Tree Names

Trees have wonderful names. Some of them are what we call "common" names. That means the ordinary names that people give to them. And then every tree has its scientific name, which is in the Latin language. Some of them are real tongue-twisters, and the way they roll off your tongue could make saying them a lot of fun. Learn the Latin names of your state tree, your favorite tree, and as many others as you like. Here are a few to try out on your friends!

Liriodendron tulipifera is pronounced "Leer-ee-o-den-drun / two-lip-piff-fur-a" (or in other words, the Tulip Tree).

Loblolly Pine is a common name, but a beaut! Lob-lolly . . . Lob-lolly! See if you can say it five times, as fast as you can — Loblolly . . . Loblolly . . . Loblolly . . . Loblolly . . . Loblolly!

24

Liquidambar styraciflua is pronounced "Liquid-amber / sty-ruh-siff-lew-uh" (in plain language, Sweet Gum).

Ostrya virginiana is pronounced "Oh-stry-uh / vir-gin-ee-anna" (it's Ironwood, one of the strongest, hardest, heaviest of all woods).

Betula papyrifera is pronounced "Bet-chula / papp-urr-if-furra" (it's the beautiful White Birch, also called Canoe or Paper Birch).

Quercus borealis is "Kwair-cuss / bore-ree-al-iss," almost like "queer cuss"! (This is the Red Oak.)

Aesculus hippocastanum is pronounced "Eye-skew-luss / hippo-cast-tin-um" (this one's Horse Chestnut).

Hamamelis virginiana is "Ham-mom-mell-iss / vir-gin-ee-anna" (our friend, Witch Hazel, ready to explode!).

Sambucus canadensis is easy — "Sam-bu-cuss / cana-den-sis" (Elderberry, but doesn't it sound like somebody's name?).

Populus tremuloides is "Pop-pew-luss / trem-ewe-loy-dees" (Quaking or Trembling Aspen, so doesn't the name make sense?).

Identification books and encyclopedias are full of Latin names for the trees. Try them out, and say them fast, for a lot of fun. If this isn't proof that Latin is a useful subject in school, what is?

LOTS OF THINGS TO DO IN THE WOODS

The woods are full of nuts in the Fall, but you've got to get there before the animals do. Squirrels tend to bury the nuts they like, and then forget where they left them. So we can thank those little furry forgetters for about half of the new nut trees that grow. If the squirrels went on strike forever, other animals would eat them without burying them, and our nut trees might become extinct.

Black Walnut and Butternut are two of the easiest to find, and the hardest to eat. They have coats of armor, and you have to crack them with a hammer and really look for the nut meat. But they're delicious once you find them. Black Walnut doesn't lose its flavor in cooking, which is why you find Black Walnut cakes, candies and ice cream. (The ordinary walnut you get in your Christmas stocking is English Walnut.)

The Hickory nuts make good eating too, if you beat the squirrels to them. Shagbark is the best, which is why Nature put up that picket fence to keep squirrels from climbing the Shagbark Hickory's trunk (see page 10). The shells are thin, the nuts sweet. If you ever see Hickory nuts in a store, they're probably from the Shagbark.

26

Mockernut Hickory is one of Nature's practical jokes. The nut looks huge, so you crack it, with your mouth watering meanwhile. But it's all shell, and just a tiny little nut in the center, and not worth the trouble! This is why somebody named it Mockernut.

Nuts for You!

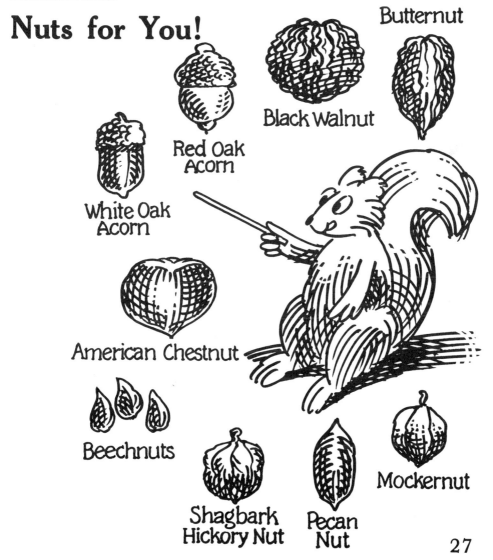

Butternut

Black Walnut

Red Oak Acorn

White Oak Acorn

American Chestnut

Beechnuts

Shagbark Hickory Nut

Pecan Nut

Mockernut

The Pecan tree is a Hickory, too, and so good that it has been tamed and now grows on farms in the South. Maybe somebody once sent your family a gift of a bag of pecans. They're delicious — in pies, too!

Beech trees grow little triangular beechnuts. They're very sweet and good, but very few people seem to find them under the Beech trees. The reason is that the birds, squirrels and deer get there first (and they get up earlier in the morning than we do!).

You've heard that saying, "Great oaks from little acorns grow." Well, some of those acorns are pretty good eating — the White Oak group. They grow from the Oaks that have rounded fingers on their leaves, with no teeth. But you have to roast them first. Be sure not to get the acorns from the Red Oak group. You can tell those trees by their sharp fingers on the leaves (known as lobes) and the bristle-tipped teeth. Their acorns are bitter. Even the squirrels don't want them.

If you've ever seen a chestnut man selling bags of roasted chestnuts in the park, maybe you wondered where he got them. Probably from Europe. The American Chestnut, a noble tree, is almost extinct. The Chestnut Blight, a disease, swept through its growing area, leaving a sad sight of acre upon acre of dead standing Chestnut trees. Our scientists are trying to revive this fine tree. Here's hoping they do, so you can enjoy the look and the taste of the American Chestnut.

28

Taste Treats in the Woods

Outside of the first things you think of — eating apples, pears, grapes, and cherries, or all the delicious nuts of the forest — Nature has a lot of other taste surprises in store for you if you just look around.

Whether you live in the North or the South, you can get some wonderful tasting chewing gum in the woods. Up north, look for either Red or Black Spruce, and pick the hardened gum off the bark. After a bit of chewing, it'll taste delicious. Southerners can pick gum off the bark of the Sweet Gum Tree, that beautiful tree with the star-shaped leaves that turn so red in the Autumn. It has a sweet, fragrant taste that is very pleasant.

The woods are full of tastes. Sweet Birch twigs, sometimes called Black Birch, taste like wintergreen. Sassafras twigs are deliciously sassafras. Honey Locust seed pods have a honey-tasting jelly inside them, and even the seeds taste like honey. Slippery Elm has — you guessed it — a slippery taste to the bark, twigs and buds. Cherry twigs are pleasantly bitter. Spice Bush twigs taste like cinnamon. And Sourwood Tree leaves (called Sorrel Tree, too) have a lemony taste that is chewed by woodsmen to quench their thirst.

Why not take a Tasting Hike next time? Especially in the Spring, when the sap flows freely!

29

Twig   Butternut   Poplar   Hickory

Look for the Funny Faces!

Ever lie back on a Summer day and watch the clouds drift through the sky, imagining all sorts of faces and shapes? Well, you can do the same thing in the Wintertime with the leaf scars on tree twigs.

Look for the Winter bud on the twig, and right below it you'll find the scar of last Summer's leaf. For this adventure, you should have a hand lens (that means a simple magnifying glass). Even the kind you find at the toy store, candy store, or as a prize in a box of Cracker Jack will do.

Inside the leaf scars are little dots that used to be the water and food pipes from the leaf to the twig. They're arranged in all sorts of funny ways to form eyes, nose and mouth. A little imagination makes the Winter bud above the face look like a hat or cap!

Here are a few that are easy to spot:

American Elm — looks like a very dull boy wearing a dunce cap. (Aren't you glad he isn't you?)

Butternut — has the face of a moose below each bud. (Make a sound like a moose!)

The Hickories — all look like various television comedians, some people, some cartoon animals.

See if you can figure out which is who!

Poplars — have very unhappy faces, as if they'd just found out that there wasn't any dessert for dinner!

Maples — aren't exactly jolly either. They look as though they've been told to stay after school!

Take a walk in the woods on a crisp Winter afternoon. Be sure you wear your boots. Find your own leaf scars and buds, and make up your own faces, just as you did last Summer with the clouds.

How to Tell
How Old a
Pine Tree Is

Once a tree is chopped down, it's easy enough to count the rings and find out its age. But this is not so good for the tree! There's another way to find out without having to chop it down. But you do have to bore into the tree with an increment borer — a corkscrew-like gadget that pulls out a core of wood.

There is still a better and harmless way to tell the age of any Pine Tree without touching it. Pines grow from one whorl (cluster) of branches to the next one in a year. During the first three years, when the tree is a seedling, it has no side branches. So, the way to tell the age of any Pine is to start at the bottom and count every cluster of branches all the way to the top. Then add three years, and you have its age.

Next time you see a Pine, stand back far enough and start counting.

C

D

Have a Sweet Balsam Dream!

Balsam Fir is a wonderful tree. Since one out of every three Christmas trees is a Balsam, you've probably had one in your house. They grow in most cool, high places in the eastern U.S. and Canada. And they're shipped all over the country around Christmas time.

Balsam is shaped like a church spire, so tall and graceful and blue-green. The bark has blisters, and if you break them, they smell really woodsy! This sticky stuff is used to cement down microscope slides. Woodsmen use it as a salve for cuts, too. (Remember "Nature's Medicine Chest"?)

Balsam needles are flat, with white lines on the undersides. They are attached to the branches with little round bases that look like suction cups, and after the needles drop off, the twig is peppered with little circular scars.

Woodsmen love to make outdoor beds of Balsam boughs, for not only do they smell good, but they're very springy. Most woodland gift shops sell souvenir pillows stuffed with Balsam needles. Better yet, fill a large bag with needles gathered from under a Balsam, and perhaps Mother would stuff an old pillow for you. Then all Winter long, you would be dreaming of the woods!

33

Staghorn Sumac

Staghorn
Sumac
Peashooter

34

Make a Peashooter

Find a Staghorn Sumac. This is easy if you live in the eastern half of the United States. It's the hairy member of the Sumac family, with velvety leaves and twigs, and big clusters of red berries.

Cut off a twig, just as long and thick as you want your shooter to be. Now simply push out the soft center section (called the pith). It's big and orange. After it's pushed out, you'll have a perfect pipe you can use for a peashooter. And, next time you want to make your outdoor charcoal barbecue burn faster, just use it to blow on the fire!

Make a Willow Whistle

(or a Poplar, Basswood, or Sycamore whistle!)

Every American boy and girl ought to make a willow whistle in the Springtime. All you need is a good sharp jackknife and a green Willow, Poplar, Basswood or Sycamore branch. One of these is available just about everywhere in the United States. Make sure you make your whistle in the Springtime, because the sap flows better then. Here's how to go about it:

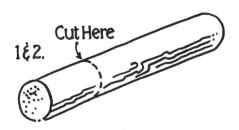

1. Cut your branch 1/2″ in diameter and 5 inches long.
2. Cut a circle down through the bark to solid wood, all around the branch, about 1 inch from one end.

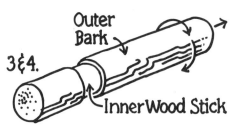

3. Now wet and pound the bark on the other 4 inches, using another stick, or the *closed* jackknife.

4. Next grasp each end of the stick with your hands, twist, and pull the stick right out of the bark.

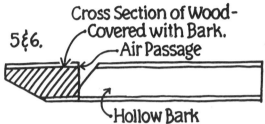

Cross Section of Wood—
Covered with Bark.
5 & 6.
Air Passage
Hollow Bark

5. Put the stick back in the bark, and cut a notch for the whistle, and a slanting cut where your mouth will go.

6. Now pull the stick out of the bark again, and cut off the end at the base of the notch. Also slice a thin sliver from the top of the plug for an air hole. Put the plug back into the bark.

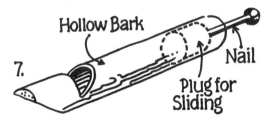

Hollow Bark
7.
Nail
Plug for Sliding

7. Now cut off a small piece of wood to plug the other end.

8. NOW BLOW! Doesn't it sound great?

Oh, if you want to change the tone, drive a long nail into the front-end plug, and you can slide it in and out like a trombone!

37

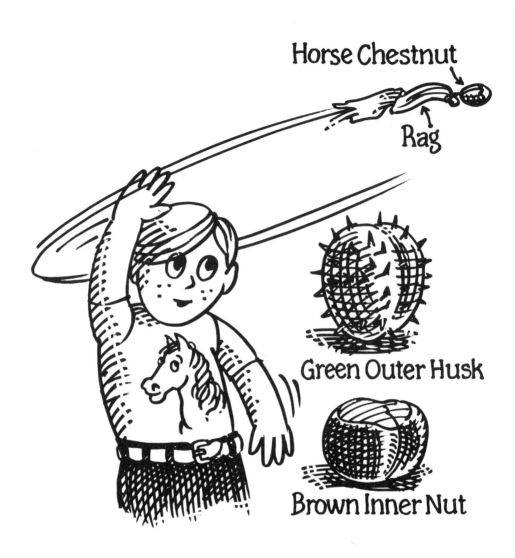

Horse Chestnut

Rag

Green Outer Husk

Brown Inner Nut

Make a Horse-Chestnut "Guided Missile"

Horse Chestnut is an immigrant to America, planted all over the country because of its beautiful flowers that look like hyacinths. The fruit has a green, spiny outer husk, so don't walk barefoot under the tree!

But it's the inner nut that we're interested in. It's a beautiful, brown, leather-looking nut with a gray eyepatch. Some people think it looks like the glossy coat of a chestnut horse.

Now for our guided missile. Take the inner nut, and bore a hole in it with your pocket knife. Tie a string through the hole, and a strip of rag at the other end. Now swing it over your head, and let it go carefully when it gets to the direction you want it to fly. You'll find you can control your homemade guided missile easily. Be sure to use it only in an empty lot, so you don't hit anybody or anything!

And if you get the idea that the Horse Chestnut nut looks yummy, forget it! It's very bitter, and you won't like it at all!

Hooray for the Mitten Tree!

If there's a tree in the woods that's more fun than Sassafras, I'd like to know about it! The first thing you see when you approach one is the rich green tone of its leaves and twigs. And then those crazy leaves that come in three different shapes — *all on the same tree!*

1. Plain oval
2. Mitten-shaped with one thumb
3. Mitten-shaped with *two* thumbs

Now, taste the tender twig — you get a spicy taste and smell that can't be described. So we'll call it sassafras flavor and let it go at that!

The roots are used for sassafras tea, and the early settlers thought it was good for practically every ache and pain they might get! Sometimes the roots are used for root beer too.

You'll find Sassafras all through the eastern half of the United States — along roadsides, and under the bigger trees in the woods.

Imagine! Three differently shaped
leaves on the same tree.

Which Tree Has Knees?

It's Bald Cypress! This stately swamp tree grows wild in the swamps from North Carolina around the Gulf Coast to Texas, and up the Mississippi Valley. But you might also see it planted as an ornamental tree in a swampy spot in a park practically any place where the winters are mild.

The Cypress "knees" are small, separate stumps or knots around the base. They help the tree to get more air into its roots. Ordinary trees in the ground get air through the soil. But, since Bald Cypress roots are sunk in water, the tree depends on its "knees" (which are out of the water) to absorb the air it needs.

The reason this Cypress is called "Bald" is that although it is really an evergreen, it sheds its needles each Fall so that it is bald all Winter. And all year-round you'll see Spanish Moss draped over the Bald Cypress, like furs dangling from a lady's shoulders.

Slippery Elm —
The Spitball Tree!

Back in the good old days of Babe Ruth and Ty Cobb, Major League baseball pitchers used a very tricky curve ball they called a "spitball." To work up a slippery surface on the ball, they'd chew the seeds of Slippery Elm.

Slippery Elm is just as it sounds — slippery. You can't even break off a twig with a snap, because the bark slips. The buds, inner bark, and seeds all feel and taste slippery. The Indians used different parts of the tree as a sore throat and cough medicine, a laxative, and even to heal sores. (See "Nature's Medicine Chest" on page 13.)

If you live in the eastern half of the United States, you'll be able to find a Slippery Elm. Look for one in the Spring, when the sap is running full, and have yourself a slippery-go-lucky time!

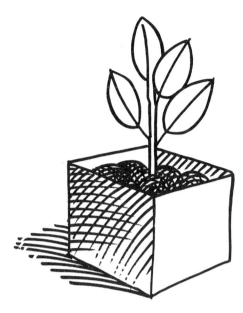

①. Seedling in container. Wait for Spring or Fall to plant.

Just for Fun, Plant a Tree!

Think about this! At Mount Vernon, where George Washington lived, there are still trees growing that he planted himself way back in the 1700's. Tulip Trees, Buckeye, Elm, Pecan, Holly, Linden, Hemlock, Mulberry. Two Pecan Trees, the oldest on the grounds, were grown from nuts that Thomas Jefferson gave to the Father of Our Country.

You can plant a tree that might grow for hundreds of years, too! Buy a small one at a nursery

② Remove seedling from container.
Be sure not to damage any little roots.

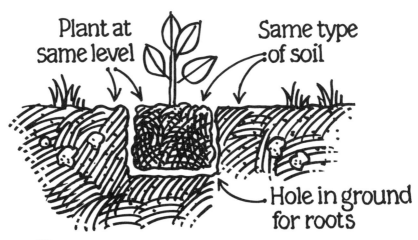

Plant at
same level

Same type
of soil

Hole in ground
for roots

③ Dig hole in ground
for your plant's new home.

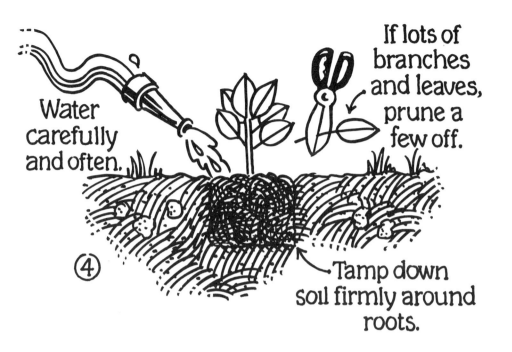

Water carefully and often.

If lots of branches and leaves, prune a few off.

④

Tamp down soil firmly around roots.

and plant it in your backyard. Or get some seedlings from your State Forestry Department. They give them away free sometimes, or for just a small charge. Get your friends to help you plant the seedlings on some ground where the soil needs holding. Early Spring or Fall is best.

It's easy to plant. Just remember to dig the hole deep enough for the roots, but not too deep. Plant the tree in the type of soil it's used to growing in. Tamp down the soil firmly around the roots. Water it carefully, and often. If there are a lot of branches and leaves, you might want to prune off a few. That way, there won't be so many using the water from the overworked root system.

V.I.T.'s (Very Important Trees)

America's Christmas Tree

Yes, there is an official Christmas Tree for all of the American people. It's the General Grant Tree, one of the largest of the Big Trees, or Giant Sequoias. It stands in Kings Canyon National Park, which is the next-door neighbor of Sequoia National Park, high on the western slope of the Sierra Nevada range of mountains in California.

The General Grant Tree soars 267.4 feet into the air. It measures 33 feet in diameter at the base, which certainly makes the annual Christmas Tree in New York's Rockefeller Center look very small indeed.

On April 28, 1926, the Department of the Interior (which operates all of the national parks through the National Park Service) designated the General Grant Tree as the nation's official Christmas Tree for as long as it lives.

Every year since 1925 (with the exception of the years of World War II) on the Sunday before Christmas, the annual Christmas service takes place at the base of this tree. Hundreds of people from near and far make the pilgrimage to Kings Canyon for this occasion.

If you live in the West, perhaps you've already seen the nation's Christmas Tree. If not, be sure to ask your family to visit it if you take a trip to California.

48

What size ornaments would you use to decorate
the Giant Sequoia Christmas Tree?

Which do you think is man's best friend?

F

The Magnificent Maples

Next to the Oaks, the Maples are the most famous of the broadleaf trees. They're found in all parts of the world, except in the tropics and the polar regions.

You'll always recognize a Maple leaf, once you've seen it, because it looks something like the palm of your hand. (Except for the leaf of the Box Elder, a Maple which has a compound leaf of 3 to 9 leaflets.) Another way to know a Maple is by the 2-winged seeds, or fruits, that we talked about under "Nature's Helicopters" on page 6. The Maple leaf is the emblem of Canada. And five of the American states have adopted the Sugar Maple as their state tree.

The outstanding Maple is, of course, Sugar Maple. It grows all over the eastern United States, except for the Gulf Coast and Florida. It gives us beauty as it grows, lovely leafy shade during the Summer, a flame of color in Autumn. It gives us maple syrup for our pancakes, and maple sugar, too. The wood is so hard that lumberjacks call it "Rock Maple," which is why it makes such fine bowling pins! It makes beautiful furniture, and you probably have a maple bedstead or chest of drawers in your bedroom right now!

Maple firewood doesn't throw sparks, burns with a nice smell, leaves a clean white ash, and the dancing flames have beautiful colors. Although they say that a dog is man's best friend, the Magnificent Maple must come in a close second!

The Tallest and Biggest Trees in the World

Up until the Summer of 1964, the tallest tree in the world (also the tallest living thing) was the Rockefeller Tree, a Coast Redwood (*Sequoia sempervirens*) growing in Humboldt Redwoods State Park in northern California. It was 359.3 feet tall when discovered in 1957. Since then, the top has been broken off by storms, so that it now measures 356.5 feet.

Then, in 1964, came the exciting discovery. Dr. Paul A. Zahl, the senior naturalist of the National Geographic Society, discovered *three* taller Coast Redwoods nearby. All were located on private property, in Redwood Creek Grove, Humboldt County, California. The tallest measured 367.8 feet, the next one 367.4 feet, and the third tallest 364.3 feet.

Why do these trees grow so tall? It's because they are nourished by a fertile soil, a heavy rainfall, and dense coastal fog.

In 1968, Congress created Redwood National Park. These three tallest trees, along with the sixth tallest, are now situated in Tall Trees Grove in the new park, and can be reached by hiking trail. Headquarters for Redwood National Park is in Crescent City, California, on U.S. Highway 101

between Eureka, California, and the Oregon border. It's an unforgettable place to visit on a vacation.

Even if you're visiting in San Francisco, you're less than an hour from some magnificent specimens of the Coast Redwood. Ask your parents to drive across the Golden Gate Bridge to Muir Woods and see these awe-inspiring trees.

Can you imagine a tree that was over 1,800 years old at the time Christ was born? It's the General Sherman Tree, the largest living thing in the whole world! (Largest in tonnage and the amount of space it takes up, *not* the tallest. Its cousin, one of the Coast Redwoods, is the tallest living thing — as it was described above.)

The biggest of the Big Trees, the General Sherman Tree, stands in the Giant Forest of the Sequoia National Park. It is 3,800 years old, and towers 272.4 feet into the sunny California sky, even though its top has been knocked off by lightning. And it's still growing!

Its eye-catching red-brown bark is 2 feet thick. As you learned on page 23, all Big Trees are virtually fireproof, disease-proof and insect-proof, so nobody knows how long this giant will keep growing. The bark has a high tannin content, which partly explains why it is so hardy. Hold your hands 2 feet apart, and try to imagine a tree with bark that thick. Then remind yourself that it's 2 feet thick on each side of the tree!

If the General Sherman Tree keeps on growing,

perhaps your great-great-great grandchildren will be able to fly around it in their *individual* rocket-driven space suits, playing with their little friends from another planet.

If sixteen grown men extended their arms and touched fingertips with one another, they would barely reach around the General Sherman Tree, which is 79 feet in circumference. In diameter, it's 25 feet through at its widest point. If it were ever made into boards (but it won't be, as long as there's a Sequoia National Park), it would make 600,000 board feet of lumber. That's enough to build eighty houses, each with five rooms! Its estimated weight is 2,145 tons, or more than 4 million pounds!

The General Sherman Tree has a *branch* alone that's bigger than nearly every tree known to grow east of the Mississippi River. Imagine, this branch is 150 feet long and 6½ feet in diameter. And it starts from the main trunk at a point 130 feet above the ground.

One more thing about the General Sherman Tree. This giant that towers more than 272 feet into the air cannot put its roots deep into the ground as does the Coast Redwood. That's because the mountain soil is just a thin layer covering solid rock. So, instead of going deep, the roots spread out, just as you spread your feet when you wrestle, so nobody can knock you over. The root system is only 8 feet deep, but spreads out and covers an area of three acres. Imagine the roots of a single tree covering three acres, or over 130,000 square feet!

The General Sherman Tree is the patriarch of the mighty *Sequoiadendron giganteum* species, commonly called the Big Tree, or Giant Sequoia. The only place you'll see Big Trees is in central California, a mile high along the western slope of the Sierra Nevada range of mountains. They are all contained in an area that is 250 miles long, and takes in three national parks — Kings Canyon, Sequoia, and Yosemite — and also some national forests.

Because these trees are mostly on federal land, they're well protected by law. But it wasn't always that way. Back in the Gold Rush days, one of these giants was chopped down, and a double bowling alley was built on its log. People came hundreds of miles by stagecoach to marvel at it, and to bowl on it.

One Big Tree that was knocked down by lightning now has a tunnel cut through its trunk, and the highway passes right through this tree. Another fallen giant has a road ramp up to it, so cars can be driven right onto it, and parked side by side. In the Mariposa Grove of Yosemite National Park, up until the early 1970's, there was a standing Big Tree with a tunnel through its base. People could drive their cars through it. Unfortunately, a severe Winter storm knocked it over.

Is it any wonder that people say you just won't believe the Big Tree until you actually see it?

The White Queen of the Forest

One of the most beautiful trees in the world is the White Birch, or Paper Birch, or Canoe Birch. Call it whichever name you wish. You can find it from the Atlantic to the Pacific, from Maine to Alaska, but not in the South or Southwest.

Its outer bark has been called "vegetable rawhide," because it's so tough. In the pioneer days, this was the source of food, drink, lodging, and transportation for those who lived in the forest. They made flour from its inner bark. Its wood was used for the rims of snowshoes. The fuzzy curlicues of its outer bark were the best fire kindler around. And its wood burned whether green or dry. Its tassels and buds were the favorite food of pheasants and partridges.

This outer bark is the famous Birch bark. It is pure white outside, and yellow-brown inside. The inner bark is bright orange. The pioneers ripped it off the tree when the weather was warm, and the sap moving. It is tough, light, strong, pliant, waterproof. It roofed the pioneer's shack, the Indian's wigwam. It was used for water pails, pots, pans, cups, spoons, boxes, writing paper. But most of all, it was used for the marvelous Birch bark canoe.

Nowadays it would be a shame to strip off this

55

bark, for we have so many other materials for the same uses. And once the outer bark is taken off, it never grows back again.

No person who loves the forest would ever strip the bark from a Canoe Birch. But if you find one that has fallen down, there are dozens of things you can make with this beautiful white outer bark. Try a tiny canoe first, and float it on the water. Write letters on it. Start your campfire with it. And thank your lucky stars that teachers don't give whippings as they did in the old days — using the branches of Birch for whipping rods!

In the famous poem, "The Song of Hiawatha," by Henry Wadsworth Longfellow, which you've probably already read in school, Hiawatha says,

> "Give me of your bark, O Birch-
>   Tree!
> Of your yellow bark, O Birch-Tree!
> Growing by the rushing river,
> Tall and stately in the valley!
> I a light canoe will build me,
> Build a swift Cheemaun for sailing,
> That shall float upon the river,
>   Like a yellow leaf in Autumn,
> Like a yellow water lily!"

In case you're wondering, Hiawatha was talking about the *inside* color of the Birch bark.

56

57

Those Wonderful Oaks

Oaks are the symbol of strength and reliability. They grow all over the world — anywhere, on dry ground, on wet ground. Their wood is strong. Their acorns are tough. They are the most important hardwood timber we have. Sometimes a sports writer will describe a mighty football player as having legs like two Oak Trees.

There are between 50 and 75 different kinds of Oaks in the United States alone. The noblest Oak of all is the White Oak, and you'll find it all over the eastern half of the United States. It grows from 100 to 150 feet tall. It is used by ship-builders and by farmers. It is used for floors in the finest homes, and for whiskey barrels. It is part of the White Oak group, which you can recognize by rounded leaf lobes (fingers) and no bristle-pointed teeth. Cut a White Oak twig in cross-section, and notice the star in the middle.

The other group, the Red Oaks, have pointed lobes and bristle-pointed teeth. The White Oak acorns mature in one season, and you can eat them, while the Red Oak acorns take two seasons and are bitter. (What a waste of time!)

White Oak Acorns (sweet)

Red Oak Acorns (bitter)

White Oaks have rounded lobes on leaves.

Red Oaks have spiny, pointed lobes on leaves.

Once you've seen an Oak leaf, you'll always recognize it. Then you'll get fooled by other Oaks such as Live Oak down south and Willow Oak, whose leaves don't even look like Oak leaves!

Down from the Dinosaurs!

It's true! The very same Ginkgo Tree that you can see in nearly every city in the country is actually a type that is 120 million years old, descended from the age of the dinosaurs. It was brought from western China, and is a favorite tree for city planting.

Notice the little fan-shaped leaves. They have veins like corn-stalks, and each has a little notch cut out of the center of the fan. Some people call this a Maidenhair Tree because the leaves resemble those of the Maidenhair Fern.

Whatever you call it, isn't it wonderful to think that you can walk past a tree that's related to the ones the dinosaurs scratched their backs against?

Go, go Ginkgo!

Dinosaur
enjoying a Ginkgo
Salad.

SEVEN FAMOUS TREES OF HISTORY

Trees seem to bring out the best in everyone. Perhaps that's why people, throughout human history, have so often selected a spot beneath a tree to make a great and solemn pact. Some may laugh and claim it was only because of the shade underneath the leafy branches. But there's more to it than just that. Stand under a mighty tree yourself. Don't say a word. Just listen to the rustling of its leaves and the sighing of its boughs. Don't you feel a little bit nearer to God?

The Washington Elm

(also known as The Cambridge Elm)

Under the graceful fan shape of this lovely American Elm in Cambridge, Massachusetts, General George Washington, the Father of Our Country, took over the command of the ragged Continental Army in 1775. Here began the long uphill struggle for American independence from the tyrant King, George III of England.

The Washington Elm lived on through war and peace, while the nation grew to a great world power. Finally, after 204 years, it died in 1923. But, because of its countless numbers of seeds, scattered over the years, its children and grandchildren will live on throughout the history of America.

The De Soto Oak

In Tampa, Florida, stood a mighty Live Oak, the species the shipbuilders prized in the days of wooden ships. The famous explorer, Hernando de Soto, after conquering Peru, was sent by the King of Spain to be governor of Cuba and Florida. He landed at Tampa Bay in 1539, and made a treaty with the Indians under the Oak that became known as the De Soto Oak.

The Indians told him about gold that could be found to the west. So De Soto and his men started west and eventually discovered the Mississippi River. Three years later, De Soto caught a fever and died. He never did find the gold.

"That's Hernando DeSoto making a treaty with the Indians beneath the DeSoto Oak."

H

The Connecticut Charter Oak

Almost a century before the Revolutionary War in which the American Colonies gained their independence from England, the colony of Connecticut grew restless. The tyrannical governor-general of New England, Sir Edmund Andros, was getting more unbearable by the year. So Connecticut petitioned Charles II, the King of England, for a charter that would give them partial self-government, which he granted them.

When Sir Edmund heard of this, he came to Hartford in October, 1687, to demand surrender of the Charter. The members of the Connecticut Assembly outwitted him by hiding the Charter in a hole in a large Oak tree. He never did find it.

So that Oak was henceforth called The Charter Oak, and became Connecticut's most famous tree. Many streets and other public places are named for it. The Charter Oak lived on for 169 years after its famous moment, before being blown over during a storm in 1856.

Exchanging wampum belts beneath the
Shackamaxon Elm.

The Shackamaxon Elm

This famous tree grew near Philadelphia, honored as the place where William Penn, the founder of the State of Pennsylvania, bought land from the Delaware Indians. It so happened that Charles II of England paid off a debt to Admiral William Penn's son, William, by granting him the territory west of the Delaware River between 40° and 43° North latitude. (A very sizable chunk of land, as you can see by looking at a map!)

One of young William's first moves was to make friends with the Indians. He wanted to buy the land from them, even though there were no laws that said he must do so. He realized that they would no more recognize Charles II's right to give away the land than the king recognized their right to keep it.

At a ceremony in 1683 marking the land purchase, William Penn and the Indian chief exchanged wampum belts under a great Elm in the Indian village of Shackamaxon. The treaty became known as The Great Treaty and the tree as The Shackamaxon Elm.

The Masonic Charter Oak

The Alamo and the Masonic Charter Oak played important parts in Texas history.

This gnarled Oak tree near Brazoria, Texas, is among the most honored trees in the Lone Star State. Under the branches of this tree, in 1836, Texas declared its independence from Mexico, and soon after conducted a successful armed revolt.

68

The declaration of independence from Mexico took place on March 2, 1836, and from that time the spot was called Washington-on-the-Brazos. Four days later, all the American defenders who had taken refuge in the Alamo fort were killed.

The Texans fought on to the battle cry of, "Remember the Alamo!" and won their independence on April 21, 1836, when Sam Houston's band captured Santa Anna, the Mexican dictator, at San Jacinto.

But why was it named the *Masonic* Charter Oak? Because exactly one year earlier, in March, 1835, six Freemasons met beneath its branches and petitioned the Grand Lodge of Louisiana for a charter at Brazoria. They were successful, and were granted the first Masonic Charter for Texas.

The Council Oak

In Sioux City, Iowa stands a huge Oak that was the scene of an historic council in 1804. President Jefferson's private secretary, Meriwether Lewis, aided by William Clark, set out to find a route to the Pacific Ocean, and to find information about Indians and the Far West. They headed up the Missouri River from St. Louis until they reached the junction of the Big Sioux and Floyd Rivers with the Missouri at Sioux City. Here, beneath the Council Oak, they held a council with the Sioux Indians to get their advice on the long journey ahead, and to tell them of their own peaceful intentions.

Cortes' Tree
of the Sorrowful Night

This huge Montezuma Cypress still stands near Mexico City. It was here that Hernando Cortes, the Spanish conqueror of Mexico, wept the night after the Aztec Indians defeated his army.

His defeat was temporary. Afterwards, he gathered his forces and marched back into battle. He won the war and became the dictator of Mexico.

Questions

TO STUMP
YOUR FRIENDS
AND FAMILY

Q. IF YOU DRIVE A NAIL INTO A TREE, WILL IT GROW HIGHER AS THE TREE GROWS TALLER?

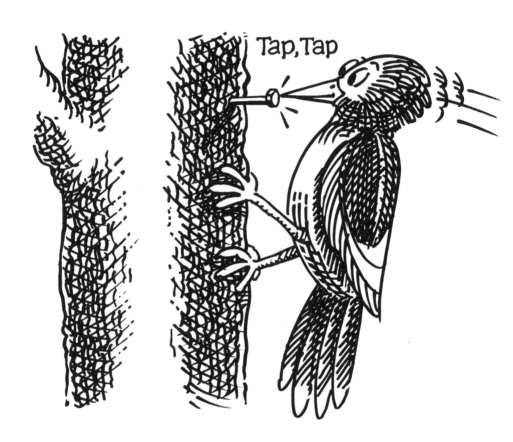

A. *No.* The tree may add growth layers to the thickness of its trunk, and add growth at the top, but it does *not* push up like a radio aerial on a car.

Q. WHICH TREE'S TWIGS LOOK LIKE RAILROAD TRACKS?

Cross-section of twig.

A. Twigs from Butternut and Black Walnut trees. (They grow nearly everywhere in the eastern United States, except in Florida and other warm areas.)

Cut off a twig with your jackknife. Now slice it the long way to expose the soft center (the pith). Notice that it is chambered with air spaces, making the cross-section look like railroad tracks with cross-ties. Butternut gives you a dark-brown railroad track, Black Walnut a light tan-colored track.

Q. WHICH TREE HAS WINGS ON ITS BRANCHES?

They may not look like my wings but that's what they are!

A. The Winged Elm, also known as the Wahoo Tree. This small Elm grows in the South, from Virginia all the way around to Texas, and through the lower Mississippi Valley. You can always tell it by the corky wings that grow along the branches. They are ridges that rise up and dip down a little like an overpass on a high-speed thoroughfare.

There's only one other tree that has anything that looks like these ridges — the Sweet Gum. And you're not likely to mix them up, because they're entirely different-looking trees. Winged Elm has typical oval Elm-type leaves, while Sweet Gum has star-shaped leaves.

Q. WHICH TREE DOES LIGHTNING LIKE BEST?

A. Lightning likes all trees, because they reach into the sky, giving it something to "ground" on. But the Oak tree is the one that's most likely to be hit in case of an electrical storm.

Scientists aren't sure why. But they think it might be because of the way the Oak's wood is formed. It has canals of resin coming out from the center to the bark, like the spokes on your bicycle wheels. This is the way a storage battery is designed.

So if you run for a tree when it rains, be very sure it isn't an Oak!

Q. WHICH TREE IS MOST RESISTANT TO LIGHTNING?

A. The Beech. Some say it's the oil in the wood of the Beech that is supposed to repel the electricity. And that this is why Beeches are struck by lightning far less than other trees. But since it only takes one hit, it wouldn't be wise to sit under any tree, even a Beech, during a storm. And, especially not if it's the tallest tree around.

Q. IS THERE REALLY A TREE CALLED THE SAUSAGE TREE, WITH SAUSAGES HANGING FROM THE BRANCHES?

Two Sausage-Pods and a Possum friend.

A. Yes, indeed. The only place in the United States where you can see this strange-looking tree is in Florida. But you'll have no trouble recognizing it. It looks like an outdoor meat market, with 2-foot "sausages" hanging from ropes. Some of these pods weigh 12 pounds. But don't try to put a slice in your sandwich, because they're very tough and inedible! The Sausage Tree is a cousin of the Hardy Catalpa, which also has a long pod (see page 82).

Q. IS IT TRUE THAT MOSS GROWS ONLY ON THE NORTH SIDE OF TREES, AND THAT, BECAUSE OF THIS, YOU CAN FIND YOUR WAY IN THE WOODS WITHOUT A COMPASS?

A. No, this is not true. Moss grows all around a tree, so you'd really be walking in circles! But moss does grow better in the shade. Since the north side of a tree in America is always in the shade, it will probably be thicker and more lush on that side.

Q. WHICH IS THE TALLEST OF ALL THE PINES?

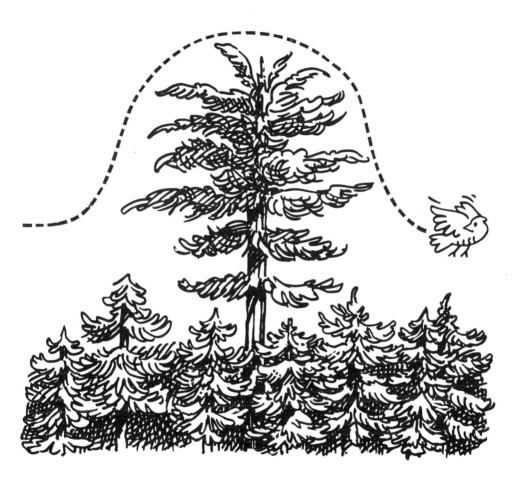

A. The mighty Sugar Pine of the Sierra Nevada range. It has been found growing to a height of over 200 feet. Its base diameter has equalled 11 feet. It has a broad, flat top, with huge branches that are bigger than most ordinary-sized trees.

Q. WHICH TREE
HAS THE
LARGEST CONES?

A. Sugar Pine again. The cones range from 11 to 24 inches long. Their seeds (or nuts) are so delicious that squirrels and people eat too many. If we don't watch out, the Sugar Pine will disappear for lack of seeding.

Q. WHICH EVERGREEN TREE HAS THE LONGEST NEEDLES?

Longleaf Pine

Longleaf Pine-needle Broom.

A. The Longleaf Pine, one of the Southern Yellow Pine group. The needles grow as long as 18 inches, in bundles of three. People collect them, tie them in bunches, and use them for homemade brooms!

This Pine is also tapped for resin which makes turpentine. The tapping is done in almost the same way as the tapping on the Sugar Maple to get the sap for maple syrup and maple sugar.

Q. WHICH BROADLEAF TREE IN THE U.S.A. HAS THE LONGEST FRUIT? THE LARGEST LEAF?

A. The same tree has both — Hardy Catalpa. It grows in the middle Mississippi Valley, but may be growing right in your town as an ornamental tree planted along the street or in the park.

Its seed pods are long, slim and black. They grow from 8 to 20 inches long, and look like big, black string beans, or long, slim cigars. The leaves are big and heart-shaped. Even the flower clusters are huge — 10 inches in height and covering the tree. The wood grows fast too — sometimes 1 inch in thickness in a year!

Q. WHICH TREE HAS THE LONGEST BUDS?

"It's either a very large bud or...a small guided missile!"

A. Beech is the winner, with long, slim buds that have been known to grow to 4 inches. They are lance-like in shape, and you could actually use one to clean your fingernails. The color is a rich brown, and the overlapping bud scales give it the look of fine, tooled leather.

Q. WHICH TREE HAS THE LONGEST THORNS (OR DAGGERS)?

A. Hawthorn (also known as Thorn Apple). This tree, though rather small, grows thorns up to 8 inches long. No wonder the birds love to build their nests in its branches, with never a worry over climbing children or cats!

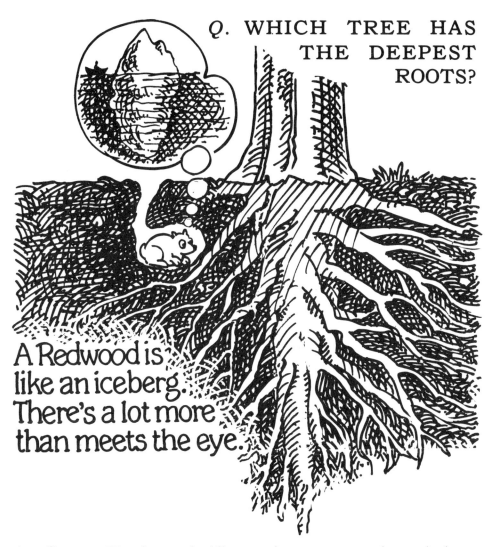

Q. WHICH TREE HAS THE DEEPEST ROOTS?

A Redwood is like an iceberg. There's a lot more than meets the eye.

A. Coast Redwood *(Sequoia sempervirens)* has roots that have gone as deep as 100 feet into the fertile soil of the Pacific Coastal Plain. (And remember, this is the tallest tree in the world, too. So you put it all together, growing up and growing down, and it's a lot of tree!)

Q. WHICH TREE HAS LEAVES THAT MAKE THE LOUDEST NOISE?

A. Trembling Aspen, one of our most widespread trees, which is found from coast to coast. Its loud leaves shake and rustle in the tiniest breeze. If you're camping out under a Trembling Aspen, it will sing you to sleep. Sometimes you'll mistake the sound for the lapping of waves on a beach.

Q. WHICH AMERICAN TREE HAS THE HEAVIEST WOOD?

A. Ironwood (also known as Hop Hornbeam). It grows in the shade, and so the rings are so close together that the wood is hard and heavy. Too hard to whittle on with a knife, but very good for tool handles. Ironwood burns slowly, very much like hard coal. You'll find it in the dry woods along the eastern seaboard from Maine to Texas.

Q. WHICH IS THE FASTEST-GROWING TREE IN AMERICA?

A. Paulownia (or Empress Tree), which was brought from the Orient during the last century, grows as much as 20 feet a year. When you figure it in inches — 240 inches, and when you note that the growing season in Washington, Philadelphia, and other eastern cities is less than 200 days, you can see that

Paulownia grows well over 1 inch a day. If you sat and watched it, do you think you could *see* it grow?

Q. IS THE WHOLE TREE ALIVE?

A. Surprisingly enough, very little of a tree is living. The whole woody trunk is dead wood except for the thin layer just inside the bark, called the *cambium*. This has the pipes that send up water from the roots and food down from the leaves. The leaves, of course, are living until they drop off in the Fall. So the entire tree is a piece of strong dead wood that supports a thin ring of living cells and tubes around the outside edge, where the water and food travel, and more wood and bark cells are manufactured. The bark, too, is dead.

Q. DO YOU KNOW YOUR STATE TREE?

A. It's fun to find out the official tree of your home state. Nearly every state picks its official flower, tree, bird, animal and song. Sometimes, two or more states share the same tree. Five different states chose Sugar Maple! What state do you live in? Find your state's tree in the list, and then look it up in another tree book or encyclopedia:

State	*Official State Tree*
Alabama	Longleaf Pine
Alaska	Sitka Spruce
Arizona	Palo Verde
Arkansas	Shortleaf Pine
California	Redwood
Colorado	Blue Spruce
Connecticut	White Oak
Delaware	American Holly
Florida	Cabbage Palmetto
Georgia	Live Oak
Hawaii	Kukui
Idaho	Western White Pine
Illinois	Bur Oak
Indiana	Tulip Tree
Iowa	Black Walnut
Kansas	Cottonwood
Kentucky	Tulip Tree
Louisiana	Southern Magnolia
Maine	White Pine
Maryland	White Oak

90

Massachusetts	American Elm
Michigan	White Pine
Minnesota	Red Pine
Mississippi	Southern Magnolia
Missouri	Dogwood
Montana	Ponderosa Pine
Nebraska	Cottonwood
Nevada	One Leaf Pinyon
New Hampshire	Canoe Birch
New Jersey	Red Oak
New Mexico	Pinyon Pine
New York	Sugar Maple
North Carolina	Flowering Dogwood
North Dakota	American Elm
Ohio	Buckeye
Oklahoma	Redbud
Oregon	Douglas Fir
Pennsylvania	Hemlock
Rhode Island	Sugar Maple
South Carolina	Cabbage Palmetto
South Dakota	Black Hills Spruce
Tennessee	Tulip Tree
Texas	Pecan
Utah	Blue Spruce
Vermont	Sugar Maple
Virginia	Flowering Dogwood
Washington	Western Hemlock
West Virginia	Sugar Maple
Wisconsin	Sugar Maple
Wyoming	Lodgepole Pine
Washington, D.C.	Scarlet Oak

WHERE TO FIND THE TREES

Everywhere you look, you see trees. On your street, on the main street of your community. In the park, on the golf course, school and college campuses, in the fields, the woods, even in the local cemetery (where trees from other climates are often brought and planted).

After you learn the trees nearby, you'll probably want to look for new trees in county parks and forests, state parks and forests, and in the

92

marvelous National Parks and National Forests. In many of these places, you'll find marked nature trails with the trees identified with tags or signs.

Sometime, you'll also want to visit the botanical gardens and arboretums where trees are growing, and the tree exhibits in museums. The following is an incomplete listing of some of these places. One may not be far from your home:

BOTANICAL GARDENS, ARBORETUMS AND PARKS

Ann Arbor, Michigan	Nicholls Arboretum
Arcadia, California	Los Angeles State and County Arboretum
Berkeley, California	University of California Botanical Garden
Boston, Massachusetts	Boston Public Gardens
Brooklyn, New York	Brooklyn Botanical Gardens
Chicago, Illinois	Brookfield Zoo; Lincoln Park
Claremont, California	Rancho Santa Ana Botanical Gardens
Coconut Grove, Florida	Fairchild Tropical Gardens
Cook County, Illinois	Cook County Forest Preserves
Jamaica Plain, Massachusetts	Arnold Arboretum (the most famous)
Kennett Square, Pennsylvania	Longwood Gardens
Lisle, Illinois	Morton Arboretum (donated by the Morton Salt family)
Miami, Florida	U.S. Dept. of Agriculture Plant Station
Montreal, Quebec, Canada	Morgan Arboretum
Muncie, Indiana	Huntington Arboretum
New Haven, Connecticut	Marsh Botanical Garden, Yale University

New London, Connecticut ....Connecticut College for
                                 Women Arboretum
New York, New York ....New York Botanical Gardens
                                (sometimes known as the
                                Bronx Botanical Gardens)
Ottawa, Ontario, Canada ....Dominion Arboretum and
                                Botanic Garden
Palos Verdis Peninsula,
    California ....South Coast
                                Botanical Gardens
Petersham, Massachusetts ....Harvard Forest
Portland, Oregon.................Hoyt Arboretum
Rochester, New York ....Highland Park
                                (a municipal park)
St. Louis, Missouri ....St. Louis Botanical
                                Garden
St. Paul, Minnesota...............Como Park
San Francisco, California ....Golden Gate Park
Saskatoon, Saskatchewan, Canada ...Forestry Farm Park
Spokane, Washington..............John A. Finch Arboretum
Vancouver, B. C., Canada ....Queen Elizabeth Arboretum
Washington, D.C. ....St. Elizabeth's Hospital
                                Grounds
Washington, D.C. ................U.S. National Arboretum

MUSEUMS

Albany, New York................New York State Museum
Chicago, Illinois ....Chicago Natural
                                History Museum
Los Angeles, California............Los Angeles County
                                Museum of Natural History
New York, N.Y. ....American Museum of
                                Natural History
Washington, D.C. ................U.S. National Museum

Once you have discovered the trees in this
book, you will want to get a good paperback book
that also helps you identify even more trees.
You'll find tree identification books in any public
library.

94

Index